Department of Health

CLEAN FOOD

Food Handlers Guide

London: HMSO

FOREWORD

Hygiene is very important to all people who come into contact with food. This guide is designed to help and remind staff of their responsibilities when handling food and the need to be ever vigilant in their personal hygiene.

May 1988
January 1990 Revised

ACKNOWLEDGEMENTS

Members of Original Working Party

Roger Armstrong	City of Bradford Metropolitan Council
Hazel O Carter	Institution of Environmental Health Officers
Jean Craven	Harrogate Health Authority
John S Neale	Brighton Health Authority
John C Reid	West Midlands Regional Health Authority
Elizabeth J Young	Suffolk Social Services (formerly DHSS)
Paul Wiltshire	Oxfordshire Health Authority
Robert E Brown	Department of Health and Social Security
Ivy D Tyler	Secretariat – Department of Health and Social Security

CONTENTS

TODAY YOU COULD KILL SOMEBODY!

BY GIVING THEM FOOD POISONING

FOOD POISONING

IS MAINLY CAUSED BY GERMS

GERMS
may be in or can get onto FOOD

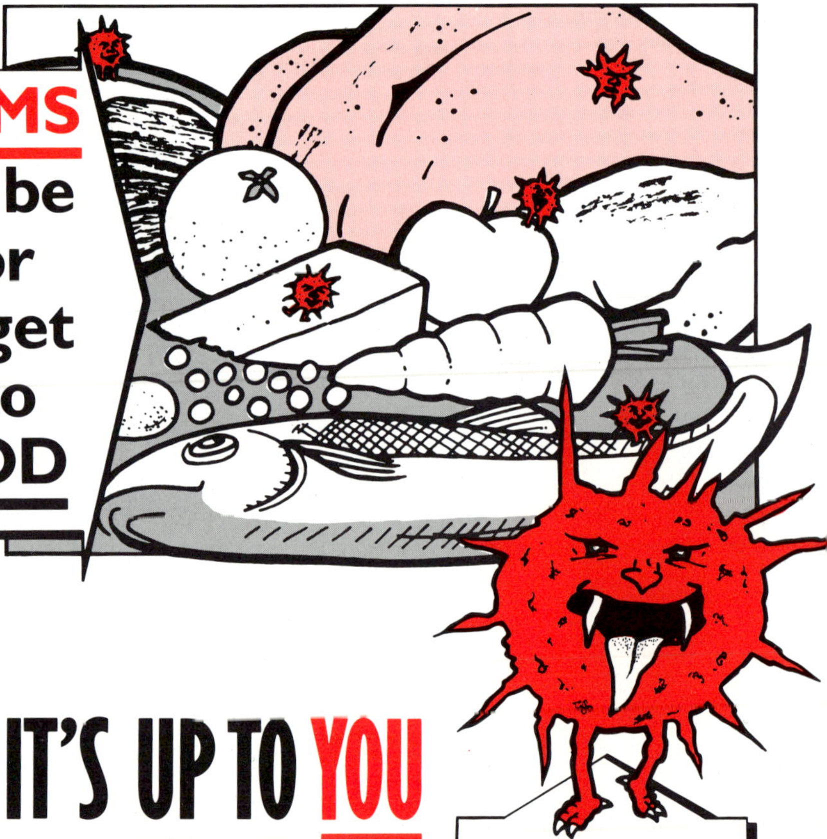

IT'S UP TO YOU TO STOP THEM

This is a GERM

GERMS & YOU

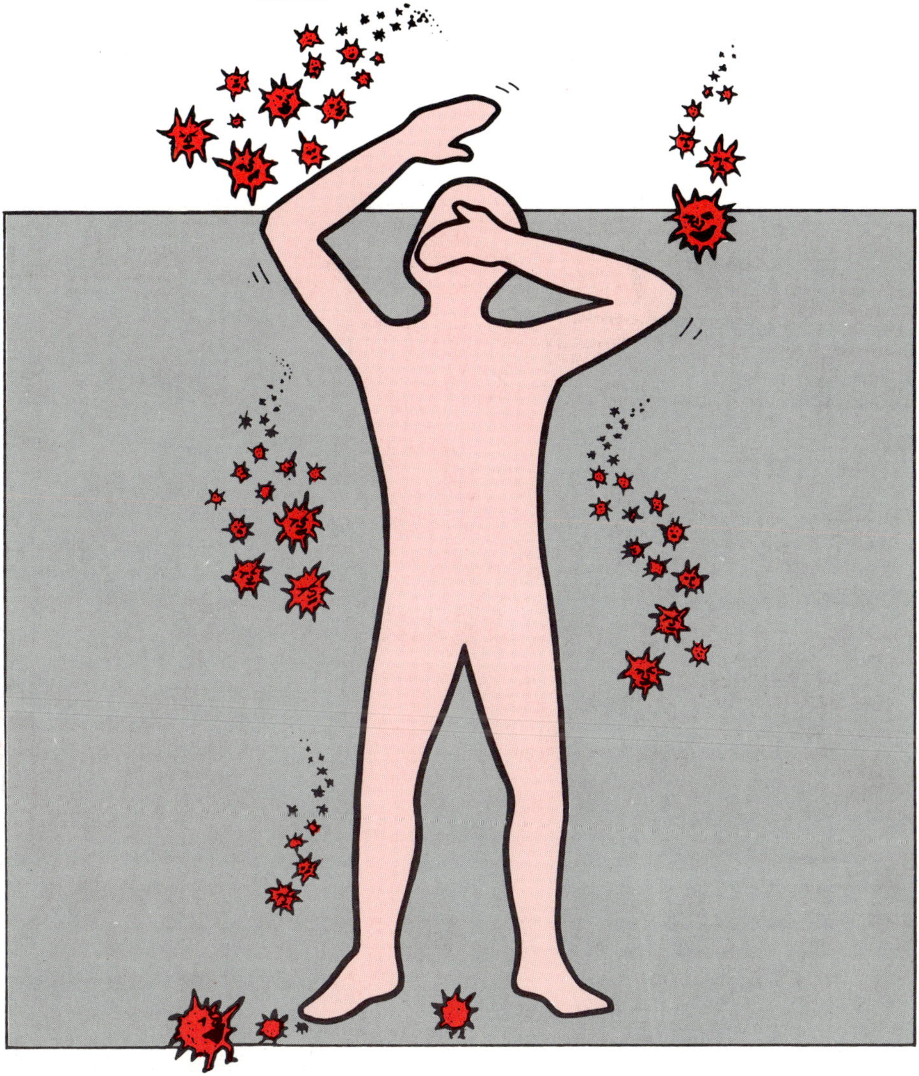

WHAT YOU CAN DO ...

PERSONAL HYGIENE

ALWAYS WASH YOUR HANDS

AFTER YOU HAVE

Been to the **TOILET**

Had a break from **WORK**

Been handling **RAW FOOD**

Handled **RUBBISH**

Used your **COMB HAIRBRUSH HANDKERCHIEF**

REPORTING ILLNESS

REPORT
to your Supervisor if you or a member of your household has...

Sore Throat · Skin Complaint · Rashes
Boils · Diarrhoea · Running Eyes or Ears
Stomach Upset · Vomiting · Jaundice

It is very Important if you have recently returned from Abroad or have suffered from an illness whilst away from work.

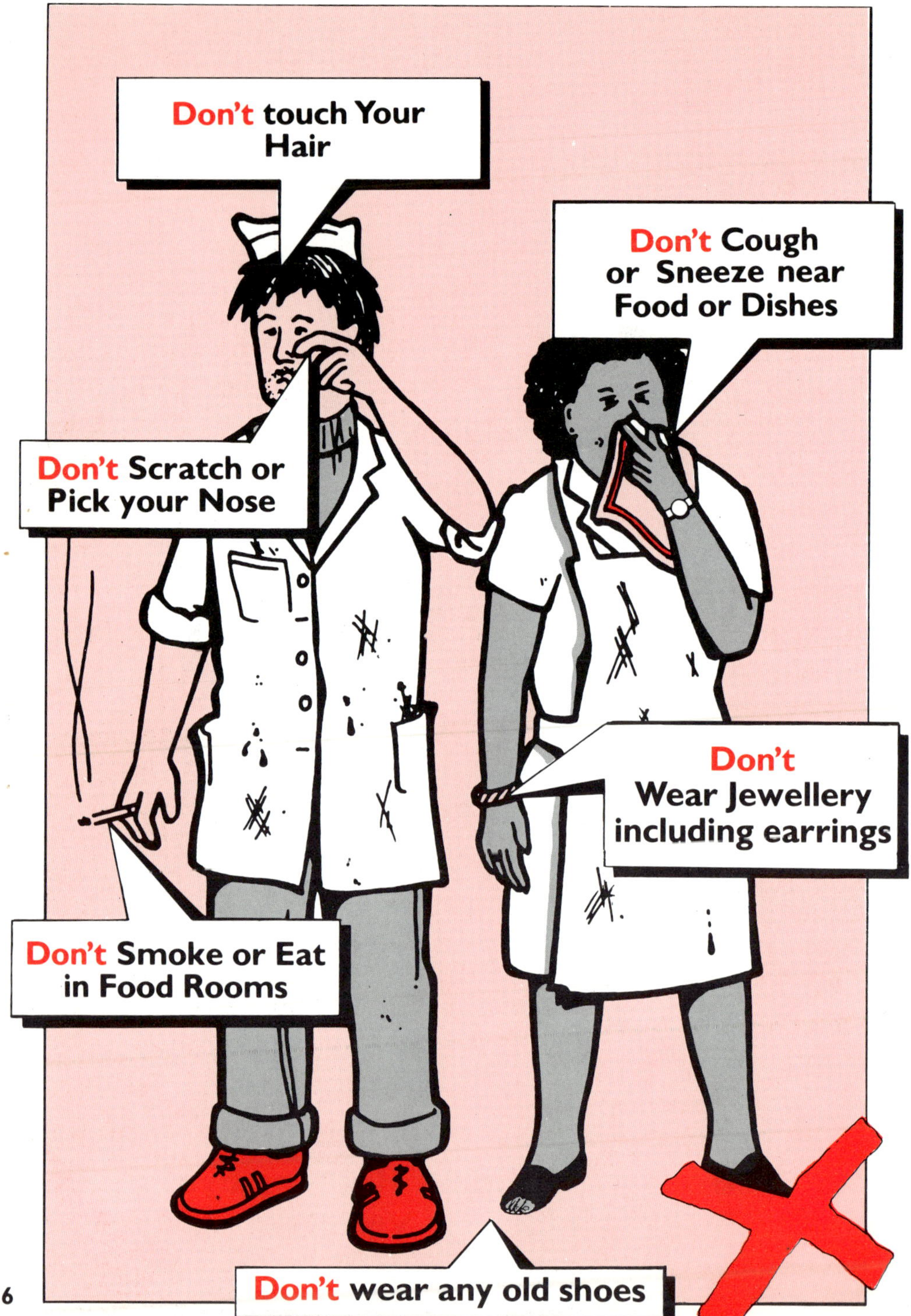
Don't touch Your Hair
Don't Cough or Sneeze near Food or Dishes
Don't Scratch or Pick your Nose
Don't Wear Jewellery including earrings
Don't Smoke or Eat in Food Rooms
Don't wear any old shoes

Keep Your Hair Neat and Covered
Wear the Correct Clothing for the Job You are Doing
Make Sure Your Clothing is Clean and Tidy
Cover Cuts and Sores with Blue Waterproof Dressing
Keep Nails Clean, Short and Free of Nail Varnish
Wear correct footwear

GERMS AND FOOD

WHAT YOU CAN DO . . .

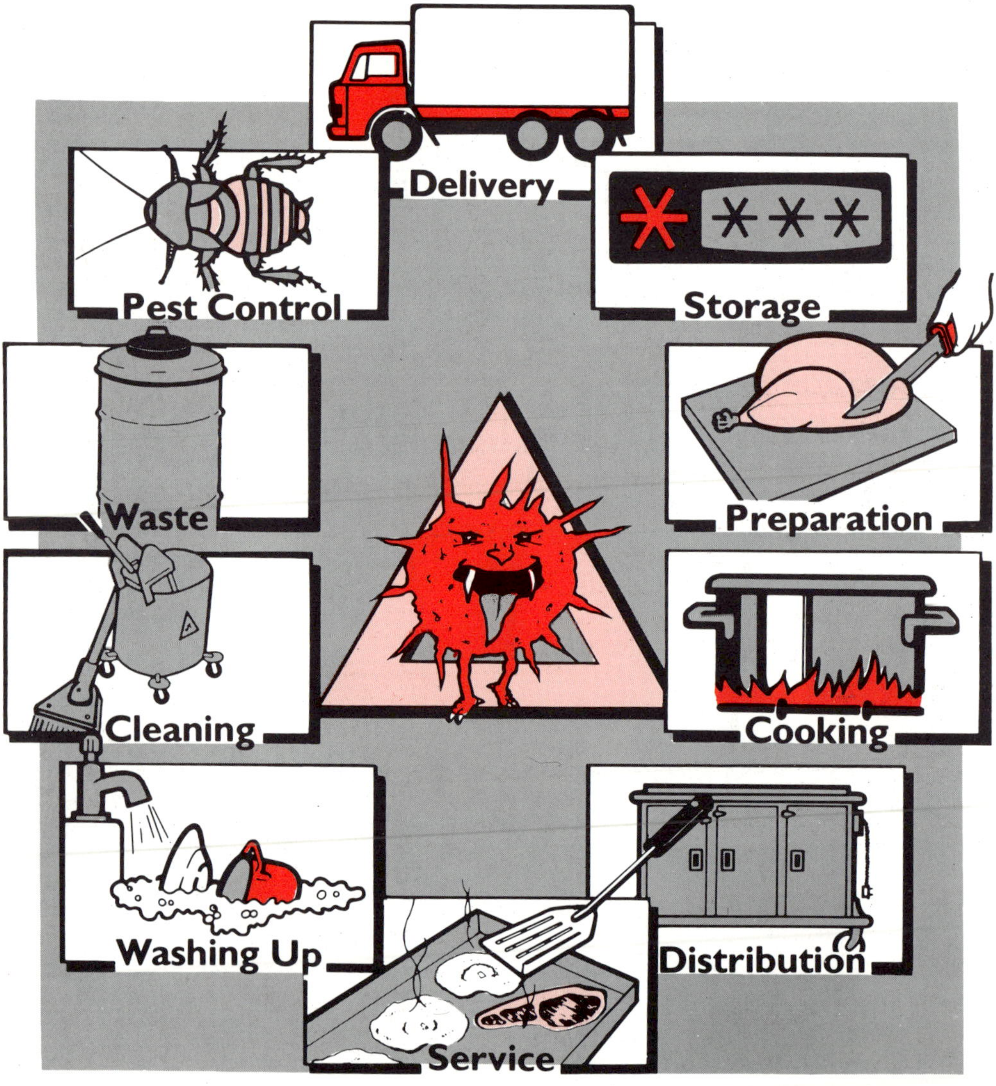

IT'S UP TO YOU TO STOP THEM

DELIVERY

CHECK GOODS PROPERLY

DO NOT ACCEPT DAMAGED GOODS

THEN PLACE UNDER CORRECT STORAGE ...

STORAGE

FIRST IN FIRST OUT

Remember! First in First Out
***OR* New in Old Out**

PREPARATION

ALWAYS WASH YOUR HANDS

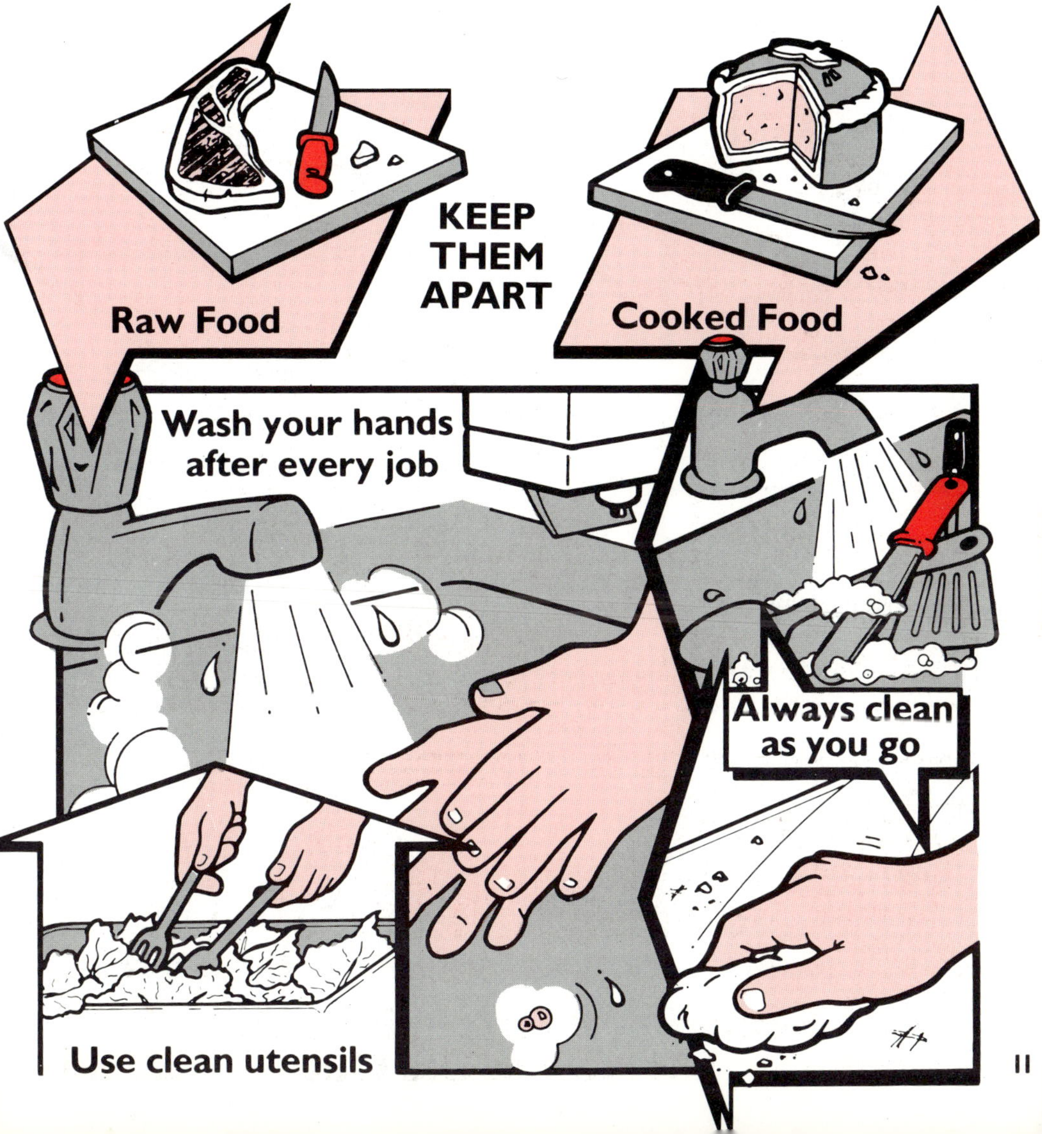

COOKING

USE YOUR SKILLS

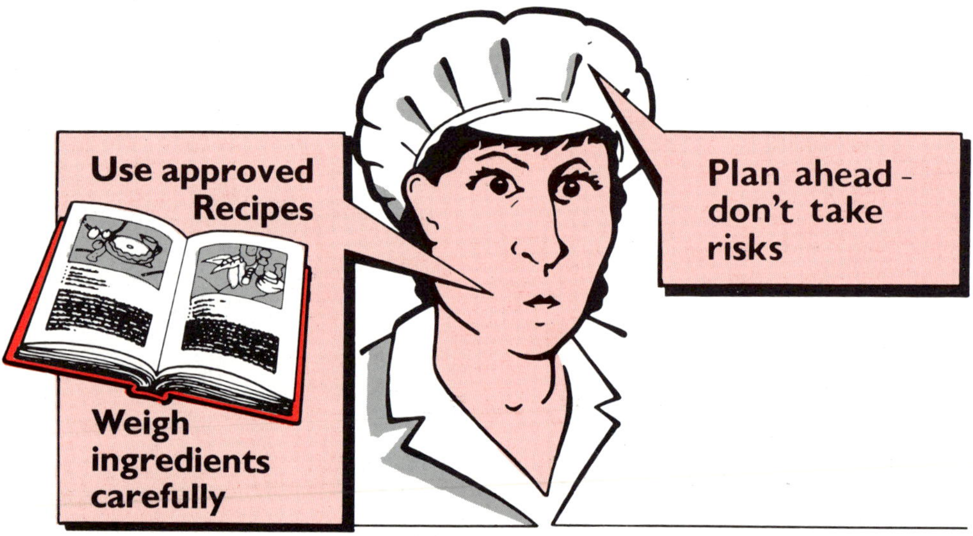

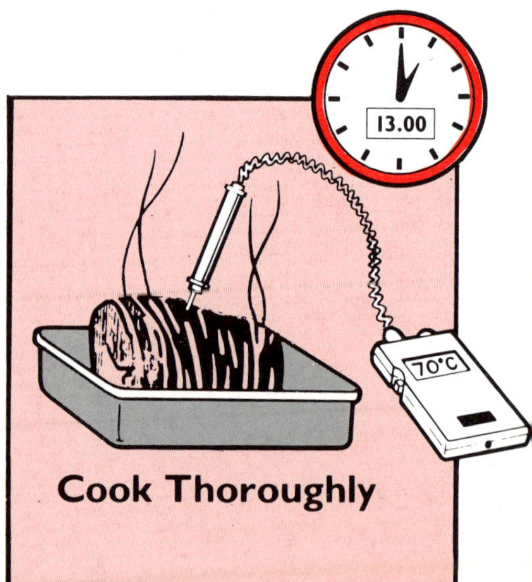

DISTRIBUTION

DELIVER IMMEDIATELY

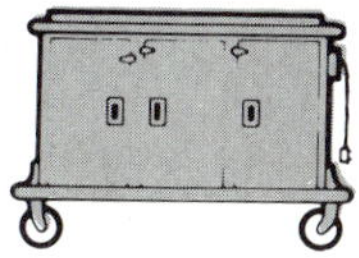

SERVE

AS SOON AS POSSIBLE

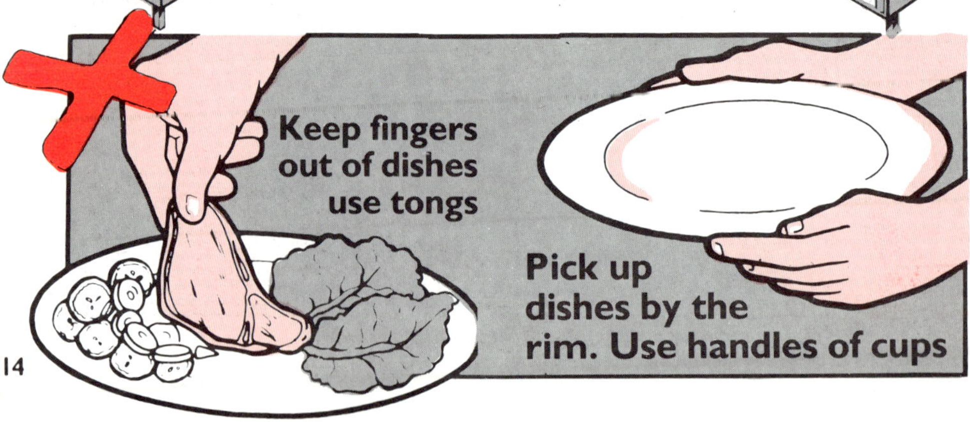

WASHING UP

USE PLENTY OF HOT WATER

CLEANING

REMEMBER! CLEAN AS YOU GO

W A S T E

KEEP AREA CLEAN & TIDY

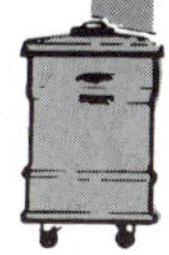

PEST CONTROL

REPORT PESTS IMMEDIATELY

Keep pests and pets out of food areas

Report any signs of Pests immediately

FOLLOW THE TEN POINT CODE

1

ALWAYS wash your hands before touching food, and always after using the toilet.

2

Tell your supervisor at once of any skin, nose, throat or bowel trouble.

3

Cover cuts and sores with waterproof dressings.

4

Wear clean clothing and be clean.

5

Remember that smoking in a food room is illegal and dangerous. Never cough or sneeze over food.

6

Clean as you go in food rooms. Keep kitchen equipment and utensils clean.

7

Keep food clean, covered and either cold or piping hot. Separate raw and cooked food.

8

Keep your hands off food as far as possible.

9

Keep the lid on the dustbin.

10

Do not break the law – Tell your supervisor if you can't follow the rules.

ALWAYS REMEMBER – FOOD POISONING CAN KILL.

Introduction

Food poisoning is an illness caused by eating contaminated food. The way our bodies react to contaminated food is by vomiting and/or diarrhoea and these are the main symptoms of food poisoning.

If you are fit and healthy you may recover in a short time, but people who are already ill, the very young, pregnant women and the elderly, may not and some may **DIE**.

Food Poisoning Germs

Although food poisoning can be caused by some poisonous chemicals and plants, **most food poisoning is caused by germs.**

What do germs look like?

Germs are living things but they are very tiny, smaller than a speck of dust. It is not possible to see them unless you use a microscope or unless you look at millions and millions of them grouped together.

In cartoons germs are made to look funny, like the germ in this booklet, but really germs can be deadly!

Where do germs live?

Germs are everywhere, in food, in water, in soil, in the air, in animals, birds and **inside you and all over your body**.

Are all germs bad?

No. Most germs are harmless and some are useful like the ones used to make yoghurt or cheese.

Some germs are harmful and they make people ill.

There are lots of different types of germs but the ones that cause food poisoning are most definitely not nice to have around and they do not necessarily alter the smell or taste of the food. Three of the most common types of food poisoning germs are:

Salmonellae	This is the most common group causing food poisoning and accounts for 80 out of every 100 of food poisoning victims.
Clostridium perfringens	This may affect from 5 to 15 out of every 100 food poisoning victims.
Staphylococcus aureus	This may affect 1 to 4 of every 100 food poisoning victims.

What makes germs multiply?

Like us, germs need **food, warmth and moisture,** and must have **time** to multiply. When germs have all this they can multiply very quickly, they just divide into two and then divide again. One germ can become two germs in 10 to 20 minutes and then those two germs can become four in another 10 to 20 minutes. To cause food poisoning germs need to be present in food in high numbers. Under favourable conditions – Food, Warmth and Moisture – one thousand germs could become one million in three hours.

What do the germs that cause food poisoning like best?

Food Raw meat, poultry, dairy products, eggs and cooked rice are good for growing germs.

Warmth Germs that make people ill grow best when the temperature is 37°C (body heat). However if we keep food piping hot or keep it very cold the germs will only multiply slowly.

Moisture Generally dried foods will not allow any germs to multiply, but if they become damp, or if liquids are added to them, then any germs that are in them could start to multiply.

Time If germs are given Food, Warmth and Moisture they will multiply as explained earlier and in a very short time they will be in large enough numbers to cause food poisoning.

Simple rules to prevent food poisoning germs multiplying on food

- Don't let germs get onto food
- Keep food piping hot or keep it very cold
- Use dried foods that have been mixed with water or milk immediately
- Don't give germs time to multiply

Personal Hygiene

What is personal hygiene?

Personal hygiene means keeping your whole body clean, especially your hands, and not making them dirty again with bad habits like picking your nose, touching your hair, and smoking.

Why is personal hygiene important?

Germs live inside you and on the surface of your body and when you touch food you may pass them on.

If you keep yourself clean and don't develop bad habits you cut down the risk of making somebody ill.

What is the best way to be clean?

It is important to wash often and use soap or gel. If you don't have a bath or shower a thorough all over wash can be just as good. Using a deodorant doesn't replace soap and water!

Will your hands become dirty at work?

Your hands are the main route for transferring food poisoning germs, they must be washed and dried frequently: **especially:**

- Before starting any work in food areas
- After using the toilet
- Between handling raw and cooked food
- Before serving food
- After using a handkerchief/tissue
- After handling refuse, and kitchen waste
- After smoking in a rest period

Remember

- Always wash your hands in the wash-hand basin, **Never** in a food preparation or washing-up sink
- Keep nails short and clean
- Don't wear nail varnish as it can contaminate food when it chips off

What about hair?

Hair should be covered or hairs may drop into the food. If you wear a beard, keep it clean and tidy.

Never touch your hair, or comb it, in a food area.

What are the habits that must be avoided?

Nose Never pick or touch your nose whilst handling food. Don't sneeze over food, people or work surfaces. Always use a clean handkerchief or tissue and don't forget to wash your hands afterwards.

Mouth Don't touch your mouth or lips whilst handling food. Don't cough over food, people or work surfaces. Don't spit.

Smoking Smoking in any food room is ILLEGAL, **Never smoke in any food room.**

If you have been smoking in a permitted area during a break period, **Don't forget to wash your hands**.

Remember when tasting food:

- Use a clean spoon each time for tasting food and wash after each use
- Don't use cooking utensils
- Don't use fingers

What about the things you wear?

Not only can germs live on your body they will also be on your clothes and on your jewellery.

- You should change your protective clothing daily
- You should only wear your protective clothing at work
- Outdoor clothing should not be brought into a food room
- No jewellery should be worn except a plain ring

Is your general health important?

Yes it is, there are times when the germs inside you find a way out and then there is a risk of them getting onto food.

Diarrhoea or vomiting If you suspect that you have food poisoning or if you have diarrhoea or vomiting you must tell someone in charge at once, whether you are on or off duty. You must also report if you have travelled abroad where you or people you live with have suffered from diarrhoea or vomiting.

Boils, Septic Spots and Sores If you have any of these you should tell someone in charge.

Cuts Any cut must be covered with a blue waterproof plaster. Some cuts on fingers may need the extra protection of a waterproof finger stall.

Delivery

The first chance you have to make sure that the food in your kitchen is in good condition is at the delivery door.

What should you look for when checking a delivery?

Does it look right?	Is the packaging dirty or wet? Are the wrappers torn or boxes broken? Are tins dented, leaking or showing signs of blowing? Is the food damaged or dirty?
Is the date right?	Is there a 'sell-by' 'use-by' 'use before' date. CHECK IT!
Is the temperature right?	Your manager should have rules about the correct temperatures of food before accepting deliveries, know what they are and use them Check the temperature of chilled and frozen food with a digital probe thermometer Probes should be disinfected after each use with an alcohol wipe

What should you do when you find something wrong?

Tell the person in charge.
Refuse to accept the delivery until it has been checked.

If the delivery is correct, What happens next?

Look at the packages for any storage instructions. Put the food into the right storage conditions straight away.

Storage

Good storage is very important if your kitchen is going to be able to serve good, clean and safe food.

There are rules which will help you make sure that food is stored properly.

- **The three C's.** Keep food **C**lean, **C**ool and **C**overed.
- Keep raw and cooked food well apart.
- Use oldest stock first.

What's the best way to store food?

There are four main groups of foods and they are stored in different ways. The four groups are: Fresh Fruit and Vegetables, Dry Foods, Frozen Foods and Perishables.

Fresh Fruit and Vegetables	Generally fruit and vegetables can carry germs in the dirt on them and should be stored away from other foods in a cool area, with adequate air circulation.
Dry Foods	These include bread, canned foods, flour and cereals. These should be stored in dry, well ventilated, cool rooms. Food must not be stored on the floor but should be put on racks and shelves.
Frozen Foods	All frozen foods should be stored in a freezer as soon as they are delivered. The temperature should be at least −18°C and this should be checked daily. Frozen foods keep better if well packed and wrapped. Food in freezers should be date marked to ensure stock rotation.
Perishables	Perishable food is food which will go 'off' quickly and should be stored in the fridge. Such food includes chilled foods, meat, poultry, eggs, fish, milk and other dairy foods.

Advice for using a fridge

There are a few rules which you can follow to make sure that you use the fridge properly.

- The fridge should be working between 1°C and 5°C.
- The temperature should be checked at least once every day.
- Food should be wrapped or put into suitable containers.
- Plenty of air space should be allowed round the food.
- Don't overload the fridge.
- Remember to close the fridge door.
- Store raw foods and cooked foods separately, but if there is only one fridge – store raw foods BELOW cooked foods.
- Don't put hot food into the fridge.
- Remember to clean the fridge weekly, and defrost if necessary.

Preparation

What is preparation?

Preparation involves taking foods or ingredients from storage and then making them ready for cooking (if they are raw) or for eating (if they are sandwiches or other foods that don't need further cooking).

How do germs get from one food to another?

Germs can be transferred from food or equipment to other food in many ways. This is called CROSS CONTAMINATION.

- By raw food directly touching other food
- By YOU touching the raw food and then touching cooked and other food
- By using equipment for raw food and then using it for cooked and other food
- By using work tops for raw food and then using them for other food
- By letting raw food drip onto other food

What are the dangers of poor preparation?

Raw food such as vegetables, meat, poultry and eggs may be a source of germs so they must not be allowed to contaminate any other food.

How do you avoid cross-contamination?

The best way is for raw food and other food to be prepared in separate areas.

- Wash all fruit, vegetables, salad items and dried fruit in cold running water in the preparation sink
- Wash your hands every time you touch raw food and before you touch food that will not be cooked again
- Use separate utensils for raw and other foods or wash the utensils thoroughly between each use
- Don't use the same cutting board or work surface for raw, prepared and cooked food. Always thoroughly clean and dry after use. Use the colour code for boards, handles of knives. For example red for raw meat, blue for fish and green for salads.
- Separate machines should be used for raw food and cooked food. Slicing and mincing machines must be thoroughly cleaned.

What happens when the food has been prepared?

If food is to be cooked	Either cook it, or cover it and store correctly
If food is NOT to be cooked	Use clean tongs or other implements to arrange it for service or cover it and store correctly until it is needed.

What about preparing frozen food?

Frozen vegetables should be cooked straight from the packet. Frozen meat and poultry must be thawed first, unless otherwise stated on the packaging.

What is the proper way to thaw frozen meat or poultry?

- Remove the meat or poultry from its wrapping and place in a container so that the liquid which comes from thawing can drain away
- Make sure that the liquid cannot come into contact with other food, utensils or work surfaces
- Thaw thoroughly in a fridge
- Take special care to ensure that the centre of the meat or poultry is completely thawed
- Remove giblets from poultry as soon as possible
- Thoroughly wash out the cavity of poultry with fresh running cold water taking care not to splash the surrounding work surfaces
- After thawing keep the food in a fridge and use within 24 hours
- After touching raw meat or poultry – WASH YOUR HANDS

Cooking

The safe cooking of food requires a lot of planning. Food must be brought to the right temperature for the right length of time.

Safe cooking requires you to:

- Use your skills
- Plan ahead
- Avoid taking risks
- Use approved recipes
- Weigh ingredients carefully
- Cook thoroughly
- Avoid cooking too soon
- Avoid storing hot food too long

Hints for safe cooking

- Hot food should be prepared and cooked just prior to service

- Food should be cooked so that the temperature at the centre is above 70°C
- Stuffing should be cooked separately
- Digital probe thermometers should be used to test the temperature at the centre of the food. Probes must be disinfected using alcohol wipes between each use
- Use a clean spoon for tasting food and wash it after each use. Never use your fingers
- Keep the size of joints below $2\frac{1}{2}$ k (5-6lb)

What happens if cooked food is not going to be eaten immediately?

So that germs can't multiply, cooked food should be stored either below 5°C or above 63°C.

Are liquids a special problem?

Large volumes of liquids like stock, gravy or soup can be a danger because the temperature may vary thoughout the pot. The liquid may be hot at the bottom and sides but only warm in the middle so germs may multiply there.

- Cook as small a volume as possible
- Use wide, low pans that match the size of the heat source
- Stir frequently – at least every 10 minutes
- Replace the lid after stirring
- Throw away any stock left at the end of the day

Is it safe to re-heat cooked foods?

You should avoid warming up food, this can make the food dangerous because as the food warms up above 5°C germs that are in the food will start to multiply.

If the food must be re-heated:

- Make sure that the centre reaches at least 70°C as soon as possible
- It should be eaten immediately
- Throw away anything left over

What about cook-chill systems?

Information on cook-chill and cook-freeze systems are in the Department of Health's publication 'Chilled and Frozen – Guidelines on Cook-Chill and Cook-Freeze Catering Systems, 1989, published by HMSO.

Distribution

Taking food from the kitchens to the restaurant servery, ward pantry or dining areas where it is to be eaten is termed DISTRIBUTION.

So that germs don't multiply in food whilst it is being taken from one place to another it is important to remember the following:

- Keep hot food hot – above 63°C
- Keep cold food cold – below 8°C
- Keep food covered.

Advice for using heated trolleys

- Clean and wash down the trolleys after each meal service
- Plug in the electrical supply and switch on the trolleys so that they pre-heat before loading to ensure the food is maintained at or above 63°C
- Load the trolleys quickly and correctly just before the time of collection
- Unplug the trolleys, deliver them immediately and plug them in again as soon as they arrive at the ward or dining area.

What about distributing cold foods?

- Cold food must be kept below 8°C

Service

Whilst food is being held for service and put out onto plates it is important to remember the following.

- Keep hot food hot – above 63°C
- Keep cold food cold – below 8°C
- Keep hands off food and dishes – keep food covered

Remember when serving food

- First wash your hands
- Wear clean protective clothing
- Use clean utensils to serve food
- Never touch the food with your hands

Advice for handling crockery and cutlery

- Keep your fingers out of dishes, cups and glasses
- Pick up – plates by the rim
  – glasses by the base
  – knives, forks, spoons and cups by the handles

Remember A separate trolley should be used for clearing away dirty crockery and cutlery.

Washing Up

Why is washing up important?

Washing up is done to ensure that crockery, cutlery, utensils and equipment are clean and free from food debris, stains, grease and water marks.

How is washing up done?

Washing up can be done BY HAND
BY MACHINE

Washing up by hand

What equipment is needed? Washing up by hand should be done in a double sink unit.

The first sink is used to remove dirt, grease and stains from crockery and cutlery. This sink must be filled with very hot water and the correct measured amount of detergent. You should wear rubber gloves to protect your hands, and a waterproof apron to protect you. Use a nylon brush or scraper to remove encrusted food.

Change the water frequently and add fresh detergent.

The second sink is used for rinsing to remove traces of detergent. Some sinks are fitted with a heater to make sure the water is very hot. This helps to disinfect the crockery and cutlery and to speed up drying. Articles should be put in racks or baskets fitted with handles as the rinsing water is too hot for handling, even when wearing rubber gloves.

If there is no heater, the water must be kept very hot by changing it frequently.

What steps should be followed? Remove waste food by scraping it into a food waste container or waste disposal unit.

Wash articles in detergent and hot water using a nylon brush, nylon scouring pads or disposable washing up pads.

Put articles in a basket or rack and place in the second sink to rinse. The rinse water temperature should be hot enough and the rinse time should be long enough to ensure air drying.

Lift out basket and leave to drain.

Leave to air dry or dry with a disposable paper towel.

Remember

- Protect your hands – wear rubber gloves
- Protect your body – wear a waterproof apron
- Check the correct amount of detergent
- Use clean cloths and scouring pads or nylon brushes
- Change the water before it becomes dirty or cold
- Drain pots and pans upside down
- Hot water makes washing up easier and hygienic, check temperatures
- Don't use wire wool
- Don't use tea towels
- Don't stack wet or damp plates use a rack

Washing up by machine

The best way of washing up is by machine. The times and temperatures of the washing and rinsing cycles are important. Make sure you check these with the maker's instructions and that the machine is working correctly, and that the correct amount of detergent and rinse aid is used. Some areas may require water softeners.

What steps should be followed?

Scrape left over food into a food waste container or waste disposal unit.

Pre-rinse articles in cold water or soak, especially cutlery.

Check the machine's operating temperatures.

Load articles into the machine correctly.

Measure the supply of detergent and rinse additive required.

Start the washing cycle.

When the rinse cycle is completed, leave articles to air dry. The final rinse temperature should be hot enough to ensure that articles are drying as they are taken out of the machine or air dry by evaporation within 4 minutes.

If necessary, finish drying with a disposable paper towel.

Check that the articles are clean.

Stack and store when completely dry.

Empty the machine after washing up and clean the jets and filters.

Cleaning

Why is cleaning important?

Cleaning is carried out to remove:

- waste food, grease, dirt and rubbish which will attract pests

Regular cleaning:

- Gives a pleasant and safe working environment
- Reduces the risk of contamination

What has to be cleaned?

So that high standards can be maintained everything must be kept clean and dry. This will include floors, walls, ceilings, lights and windows as well as working surfaces and equipment.

How should cleaning be done?

You should follow a planned cleaning programme which will tell you what to do. This will show:

- How often cleaning should be done
- What has to be done
- Who has to do what
- What cleaning materials to use
- What cleaning equipment to use
- How to do the job
- Any special safety measures
- Who will check the work

What are the most important things to remember?

- Only use cleaning materials for the correct job, read the instructions on the label.
- Only use detergent in the correct strength and **Never** mix cleaning materials.
- **Always** use separate colour coded equipment, gloves, cloths for cleaning toilet areas.
- **Always** wash your cleaning equipment after use in the cleaners sink. Never in the kitchen sinks.
- Store your cleaning equipment and materials in the correct place.
  Never in a food room.

Waste

There are two kinds of kitchen waste, **food waste** and **refuse.**

- Food Waste : includes trimmings, plate waste
- Refuse : paper, plastic, cans, bottles, aerosols

Why is it important to store waste properly?

If waste is not stored properly it can:

- Cause unpleasant smells
- Attract pests

How is waste stored?

You should always put food waste and refuse in separate colour coded containers. If the refuse is going to be incinerated it is important to put glass and aerosols in a separate container.

Disposal of waste

What types of containers should be used?

Food waste indoors

The best way to get rid of food waste is in a waste disposal unit but if there isn't one, then:

- Make sure that food waste is placed into a smooth, easily cleaned container with a self closing or tight fitting lid
- Disposable bin liners can be used but you should secure and remove them when $\frac{3}{4}$ full
- You should empty containers regularly and clean and dry them at least once a day

- You must not leave waste in a food room overnight
- You must always wash your hands after handling waste.
- When removing sacks of waste avoid taking them out through clean areas such as the cooking or preparation rooms.

Food waste outside

Food waste must be removed from all food rooms and stored outside for collection.

- You should put the food waste in closed, tightly lidded containers. Protect plastic sacks by putting them in bins.
- Bins should be stored off the ground
- Containers should be emptied and washed after use
- You should keep the area tidy and wash it down regularly
- You must always wash your hands after handling waste

Refuse

- Refuse should be kept in pedal operated bins with strong disposable liners.
- Bins should be emptied at least daily and cleaned inside and out frequently.
- Outside the food preparation area, refuse should be kept in bins with tight fitting lids.

Remember

- Wash your hands after handling waste food and refuse.
- The equipment that you use for cleaning bins and refuse area must not be used anywhere else.

Pest Control

A kitchen and its storage areas attract pests like cockroaches, flies, ants, rats, mice, cats and birds. They have everything they need, food, warmth and shelter. All of them are pests because they can damage food and buildings and can carry dirt and germs to food.

How do pests get into kitchens?

Pests can be carried into food rooms with incoming deliveries or can be attracted by the smell of food. Domestic animals may be attracted because people feed them.

How can you tell if there is a pest problem?

You should look for signs of infestation.

- You should report any signs of pests to the person in charge.
- Inspect dried foods regularly and if infested the supervisor should be told.
- You should store packets of food tidily so that you can check more easily for the pests themselves or for signs of them, for example, in the case of mice you should look for droppings and damage to packets and woodwork.

How can you discourage pests?

Pests can be controlled and kept out of food rooms if everyone is alert and careful. Pests can find enough to eat in the bits of food that are left lying around if you don't clean up properly. Pests can get into waste bins if you don't put the lids on properly.

Cats and birds can become pests, so don't encourage them.

Printed in the United Kingdom for HMSO Dd 290286 C500 2/90